HAMSTERS
AS A NEW PET

by Anmarie Barrie

© Copyright 1990 by T.F.H.

CONTENTS

Photos by Dr. Herbert R. Axelrod, Isabelle Francais, Ron and Val Moat, Michael Gilroy, Penn-Plax Plastics, and Burkhard Kahl.

Published by
T.F.H. PUBLICATIONS, INC.,
1 TFH Plaza,
Neptune, N.J. 07753
Made in the USA.

INTRODUCTION

The golden hamster, whose scientific name is *Mesocricetus auratus*, is today probably the most popular small pet in the world. This is somewhat surprising in view of the fact that it is (to rabbits, mice and guinea pigs) comparatively a 'new' pet having been known to the Western world only since the late 1930s, indeed not in the USA until after World War II.

The golden hamster, as opposed to other hamsters, was originally described and named by Waterhouse in 1839, but thereafter it seems to have vanished, as though extinct—which, by some, was thought to be the case. However, a Dr I. Aharoni was on expedition near Aleppo, on the Euphrates river in northern Syria, during 1930, and succeeded in capturing a female and her 12 babies from their den some 2.5 m (8¼ ft) below the ground. These were sent to the Hebrew University in Jerusalem where Aharoni and his daughter conducted a breeding program which resulted in a very viable nucleus of stock within one year. Stock was sent to the UK in 1931 and to the USA in 1938.

The hamster was, and still is, used as a laboratory animal and it was no doubt through this that examples became known and available to the public. Just after World War II, the National Hamster Council was created in the UK and this, together with the hamster's great virtues, soon saw people clamoring to own these pets.

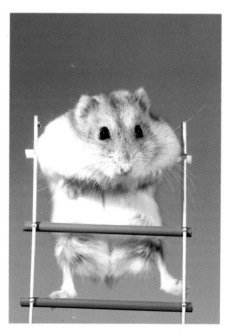

Hamsters are active, attractive pets and have become one of the world's leading pet animals. Their cage should contain sufficient exercise possibilities as the animal is naturally curious and investigates everything. This cute fellow is climbing a ladder to nowhere.

Why are they so popular? The reasons are numerous. Firstly, and this fact is of immense importance, is that the hamster does not possess a tail, only the rudiments of one. Now, this might not seem important to most children, but to millions of *mothers*, it can make the difference between their children being allowed a pet or not! Many women, though by no means all, cannot stand anything that *looks* like a mouse or rat, both of which have had very checkered histories as pets. A hamster is cute, cuddly, cheeky, and with that sort of combination it quickly made its way to stardom. It is almost odorless, quiet, easy to feed, and available in a whole range of colors and coat patterns; today there are also long-haired, rex, and satin-coated hamsters, so that this little rodent has just gone from strength to strength with its admirers.

A hamster is easily accommodated in the home—a big advantage over rabbits and guinea pigs, which invariably live outside, or in a shed. The hamster is thus available indoors for the children to play with and watch as it goes about its daily routine. People will happily look after a hamster when you are on vacation; they are less keen on a mouse or rat. Nor is it just children who own hamsters as, with so many varieties to choose from, there is almost a cult following of adults who both breed and exhibit their stock, of which they are justifiably proud when it gains honors.

In this book, we shall look at every facet of the hamster from its life in the wild, its relatives, through accommodating and looking after it.

Exercise wheels are available from your petshop. They come in many varieties. It is necessary to give your pet hamster the opportunity to exercise.

QUICK GUIDE TO HAMSTERS

Golden Hamster Country of Origin	Syria
Scientific Name	*Mesocricetus auratus*
First Named	1839
First Seen in USA UK	1938 1931
Animal Class	Rodentia
Number of Hamster Species	Approx 14
Longevity	Up to 3 years, longer in other species (possibly)
Dental Formula	$\dfrac{1\text{-}0\text{-}0\text{-}3}{1\text{-}0\text{-}0\text{-}3}$ = 1/2 jaw = 16 teeth
Adult Weight (average)	120 grm (4.2 oz) Female 108 grm (3.8 oz) Male
Digits – front and rear	4 – 5
Rectal Temperature	36 – 38°C (98 – 101°F)
Breeding Season	Continuous
Estrus Cycle	4 days but can be 5
Gestation Period	16 ($\pm$1)
Litter Size (Normal)	6 – 8 but can be 2 – 16
State of Young at Birth	Naked & Blind – eyes open approx 12th day onwards
Age at Weaning	21 days approx
Sexually Mature	6 – 8 weeks
Upper Breeding Age	Female 18 months, male life
Number Colors & patterns	Approx 32 plus 4 coat types

NATURAL HISTORY

The golden hamster, *Mesocricetus auratus*, is a member of the highly successful mammalian order known as Rodentia, the rodents, so named because of their gnawing front teeth, called incisors. If looked at in terms of number of species, distribution range, and adaptation to various ecological environments, rodents are the most successful mammals on earth. One member, the rat, is second only to insects as the most feared, hated, and hunted animal with which man has to contend.

Rodents are found on all continents except Antarctica, and they range in size from the diminutive African dwarf mice at only 8 cm (3¾ in) to the largest rodent, the capybara of South America, which is about 1 m (3 ft 3 in) in body length. However, most are quite small. Rodents can be found in deserts, tropical forests, frozen wastes, open plains, and in or by rivers and lakes. Exactly how many species there are is open to considerable debate and numbers from 1,500 to 3,000 will be seen in various books, the former possibly being nearer to the truth; either way, no other order of mammals compares with them on this account.

Evolution

All rodents are believed to have their phylogenetic roots in the Tertiary period of the Cenozoic era and can be traced to the lower Eocene epoch, about 54 million years ago. At that time there lived the first rodents which were known as *Paramys* and from these developed a progressively larger number of rodents, each radiating out and creating new species on a continuum basis. The largest of all rodents appeared about the Pliocene epoch (7-2 million years ago) and this enormous one was as large as a hippopotamus! However, the success of the group was clearly with much smaller animals which continued to speciate as the years rolled on.

What is a Rodent?

No animal can be identified by a singular diagnostic feature but rodents come close, although they show great variation in common—the arrangement of their teeth. All rodents possess four incisors located at the front of the jaw. There are two above and two below, the latter just behind the former. These four teeth grow continually throughout the animal's life so that if they are not aligned correctly, or if one fails to appear for any reason, then its opposing tooth will continue to grow, up or down as the case may be, and will eventually grow right through the opposing jaw, causing death through starvation.

It can be mentioned that rabbits and hares have eight incisor teeth in a four-paired position (one tooth behind the other); thus they are not rodents, as it is often thought, but are in a related order known as Lagomorpha.

The teeth of rodents have enamel only on their front edges. The molars of most rodents, including hamsters, are not continually growing and slowly wear down as the animal ages. There are no canine teeth in rodents; instead, there is a gap between the incisors and the premolars (if present, which they are not in hamsters)

Dormice, like the one shown here, are closely related to the hamsters and are slowly becoming increasingly available as pets.

6

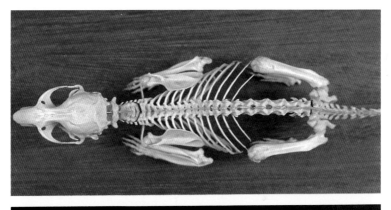

which is known as a diastema. Rodents can move their lower jaw forward, backward, and sideways; this gives them the ability to gnaw, grind, and masticate their food. The dental formula of the hamster is $1\text{-}0\text{-}0\text{-}3 \div 1\text{-}0\text{-}0\text{-}3 = \frac{1}{2}$ jaw = 16 teeth.

Rodents are divided into four suborders and the hamster belongs to that known as Myomorpha, which is the largest of these suborders.

Suborder	Examples of this Group
Bathyergomorpha	African mole rats
Hystricomorpha	Coypunutrias, agoutis, porcupines, pacas, chinchillas, cavies (guinea pigs)
Sciuromorpha	Squirrels, prairie dogs, marmots, beavers, pocket gophers, kangaroo rats
Myomorpha	Rats, mice, jerboas, hamsters, voles, lemmings, muskrats

Note: Authorities differ on the classification of the rodents and the above suborders are based on those proposed by Sir John Ellerman in 1940 (*The Families and Genera of Living Rodents*)

The myomorphs are composed of a number of families and the one of interest to us is Cricetidae. Among the many other genera, Cricetidae includes the hamsters. All hamsters are small in size and most have cheek pouches in which to store food. They have four digits on their front feet and five on the rear, and their dentition is typically that of rodents.

Hamster Species

In the past, books devoted to hamsters have always been restricted to coverage of the golden hamster. However, as a genera group, they are rarely detailed, yet one or two offer interesting possibilities for the future; indeed, some are already seen on occasion. I will therefore briefly review the group so as to provide a platform on which further information can be researched by those interested in the other species. Because a number of them are superficially similar, there is always the risk that attempts might be made to hybridize species. This has little to offer the fancy as species are always better kept pure. This has practical merit inasmuch as one or two species are more sociable with their own kind than are others. If this fact is not fully appreciated and one of the social species became popular, there would be the serious risk that people might mix one with the other, incurring disastrous results for the hamsters.

Size

The smallest hamster is the striped hairy-footed *Phodopus sungorus*, which ranges from 5.5-10.5 cm (2¼-4 in) in body length and can have a short stub tail of about 1.25 cm (½ in) in larger specimens. The largest species is the common hamster, *Cricetus cricetus*, which will attain a body length up to 34 cm (13½ in)

The smallest hamster is the striped hairy-footed hamster, *Phodopus sungorus*.

These are Chinese hamsters in a 1 oz. shot glass. Chinese and other exotic varieties are becoming increasingly popular.

and a tail to 6 cm (2¼ in); this is a very large hamster which will be discussed further.

The golden hamster, as sizes go, is in the larger ranges, being about 18 cm (7 in) maximum in wild stock, but somewhat smaller in the popular domestic varieties. This may well have stemmed from the high degree of inbreeding that was practiced when species was first being established in captivity.

Habitat

The vast majority of hamsters prefer semi-desert type conditions but there are two exceptions. The mouse-like hamster, *Calomyscus bailwardi*, is the only member of its genus and lives on mountains up to 5,000 meter levels. It is unusual in that it sports a long tail, which is greater in length than its body of 8 cm (3 in); further, it has no cheek pouches and is considered a transitional species, linking the hamster to the New World white-footed mice. The other hamster which has adapted to unusual habitats is the rat-like hamster, *Tscherskia triton*. This species, more resembling a water vole than a hamster, prefers moist areas and is found near rivers in China. It can attain a body size of 18-25 cm (7-10 in).

Most species of hamster will happily live in cultivated areas and in fact some are regarded as pests due to the large stocks of grain, beans, and potatoes they will take and hoard.

Hoarding

This characteristic of most hamsters is also typical of many other rodents— squirrels are famous for it. The level of hoarding can be quite amazing and reaches its peak in the large common hamster which can store up to 50 kg of mixed vegetables in a year. Even the small hamster, *P. sungorus* can deposit about 200 g in its den, equalling about a six months supply. Ironically, such hoardings are rarely eaten over winter as the hamsters are very thrifty creatures and always store much more than is needed.

Diet

All hamsters are primarily vegetarians and secondarily carnivores, the latter usually being restricted to small invertebrates such as insects and their larvae; however, the larger hamsters will kill small field mice if the opportunity presents itself, and will be regular eaters of earthworms.

The hazel dormouse,
***Muscardinus* sp.**

Burrows and Dens

The extent and depth of burrows varies considerably among hamsters, but as a general rule, those of the smaller species are found nearer to the surface than those of larger species. They are also less complex in small species that are not averse to sharing the burrows of other rodents, off which they excavate their own little chambers.

Hamsters do, in fact have two types of home; one is a much simpler affair which is used during the summer months when food is plentiful while the other, deeper variety, is for winter. In these, the entrance holes are filled in during especially cold periods and the hamster is thus quite snug, with more than enough food to tide it over until the weather improves. Only the living quarters are lined with grass, fur, and other materials. Entrance holes will be numerous and invariably will be at an oblique angle or nearly vertical (the smaller species in particular favoring the vertical).

Hibernation

Hamsters do not hibernate in the strict sense of the meaning but purely 'close down' a number of systems, such as breathing and heartbeat rate, for short periods of up to seven to ten days. During this period, they are termed "torpid". This condition is seen in the pet hamster if the temperature drops.

Color

The typical hamster color can range from light sandy brown to dark brown with

Longhaired or Angora hamster.

gray and even black on the flanks and back, and gray or white on the underbelly. Albino forms are known, as are melanistic (black) examples, especially in the common hamster. The striped hairy-foot hamster, which is found from eastern Europe through southern USSR to China and Mongolia and south to Turkey, exhibits a color phase in the more northerly regions of its distribution and becomes almost white with the onset of winter. This species, which is normally nocturnal, also becomes diurnal (active during daylight hours) during the winter period.

The striped hairy-foot hamster is also known as the Russian, Dzungarian, or Dwarf Russian hamster and in the same genus is Roborovsky's hamster, *Phodopus roborovsky*. Both species are gray-brown in color and have a central black stripe down their backs, and further black arches on the paler flanks. Roborovsky's hamster is somewhat smaller than *P. sungorus* and also has two small white spots over the eyes. Both are white to gray

on their undersides and are sometimes available to hamster enthusiasts. The species is far less aggressive towards its own kind than many hamsters and groups can be kept in reasonable harmony, but the size of the accommodation is crucial, and must be spacious.

Sociability

Most hamsters are solitary creatures but it has been shown that *Phodopus* species are less aggressive than most. Another species that has a similar predisposition to being friendly with its own kind is the short dwarf hamster, *Allocricetulus curtatus*, and its related species, the Eversmann's dwarf hamster, *A. eversmanni*. These are both of similar size to the golden hamster but are probably

13

more reliable in temperament. This is true of any animal which is more social with its own kind.

Breeding Behavior

In the non-social hamster species, the normal mating procedure is that the male will enter the female's burrow which will be marked by the male with scent from its special glands. The female is always wary of the male and initial contact is by mutual sniffing of the air—the female often hissing and striking at the male. However, the male will avoid such attacks and pursue the female. Eventually she will allow him to catch her and copulation takes place.

This cinnamon-colored hamster has been a favorite color in Ireland.

Thereafter, the female will again become aggressive and chase the male from the burrow after one or two days.

There are still aspects of the social and breeding lives of hamsters that are yet to be fully researched for it has been shown that a pair of common hamsters, normally solitary animals, will not only remain together, but will breed and rear young together. The first person to report this was Rosl Kirschofer in 1950.

Interspecies Compatibility

I can find no information that would suggest that hamsters will mix with each other, even where their ranges overlap, so it is not recommended that species be kept together; further, hamsters should certainly not be kept with other rodent species such as mice or gerbils as this is to risk bitter fighting and probably the death of one or other of the animals.

The only other genus not so far mentioned is that of *Cricetulus* which contains five species. Of these, the Chinese hamster, *C. griseus*, is sometimes offered for sale.

This is a gray-brown coated hamster with a black band down its back; however, this may be missing and the species may be confused with the striped hamster, *C. barabensis*, which is very similar, and always carries the stripe.

This chapter would not really be complete without further reference to the oldest known hamster, the common *Cricetus cricetus*, which was named by Linnaeus in 1758. It is found throughout many parts of Europe and extends to Africa, Russia, and Asia. It is not only the most documented of the hamsters, being referred to in literature as long ago as 1679, but also is one of the most distinctly colored, being largely black-brown on its back, and having lower cheek, shoulder, and thigh areas in white and yellow which contrast with the all-black belly. The head is light brown with patches of gray-white. It has been ruthlessly hunted over the centuries not only for its fur but because of its crop-raiding lifestyle. It has acquired a reputation for being very aggressive yet those who have reared them from babies claim they are extremely intelligent, very playful, and tamable animals.

The hamster enthusiasts will find that further references to the hamsters of the wild will be most rewarding and may bring to light aspects and species they knew little about.

This is a dominant spot Chinese hamster.

15

HAMSTER SPECIES

Genus/Species	Size(Including tail) (Average)	Distribution (General)
Calomyscus		
C. bailwardi (Mouse-like hamster)	16.5 cm (6-1/2 in)	Afghanistan, Iran
Phodopus		
P. sungorus (Striped hairy-foot; Russian; Dzungarian)	9 cm (3-1/2 in)	USSR, China, Mongolia
P. roborovskii (Roborovsky's)		
Allocricetulus		
A. eversmanni (Eversmann's)	16.6 cm (6-1/2 in)	USSR, N. China
A. curtatus (Short dwarf hamster)		China
Cricetulus		
C. barabensis (Striped)	13 cm (5 in)	USSR
C. griseus (Chinese hamster)	12.5 cm (5 in)	SW, USSR, N. China
C. longicaudatus (Longtailed)	16 cm (6-1/2 in)	USSR, Mongolia, China
C. migratorius (Migratory hamster)	13.5 cm (5-1/4 in)	Bulgaria and east to China
C. lama (Tibetan)		Tibet
Tscherskia		
T. Triton (Rat or vole-like hamster)	26 cm (10 in)	S. China
Cricetus		
C. cricetus (Common hamster)	32 cm (12-1/2 in)	Europe east through USSR and N. Asia
C. c. nehringi (Rummanian hamster)		
Mesocricetus		
M. auratus (Golden hamster)	18 cm (7 in)	Syria

HAMSTER VARIETIES

Since the original golden hamsters made their appearance as pets, many mutations have appeared and been fixed into the species. Such mutations have not been restricted to the color of the hamster as there are many variations to the coat patterns—the way in which the colors are placed on the hamster. The third type of mutation that has been developed is in respect to the fur itself, so that by combining each of these varieties it is now possible to produce a very extensive range of hamsters—so much so that most breeders will specialize in just a few of the colors and coat types.

What is a Mutation?

All animal species have developed through a continual process of small changes that enables them to see if those changes are beneficial to them. The exact cause of these changes, or mutations, is not fully understood, but it is believed that they are caused by cosmic rays, radiation or similar; these rays cause certain genes to change the way in which they express themselves. Under wild conditions, few such changes benefit the population and so never become established—though they may remain in a heterozygous state for generations, until the animals carrying them eventually all die from one cause or another.

When any species becomes continually bred in a

A Chinese hamster and his exercise wheel.

17

them, so that the older the mutation the better the quality, overall, of the hamster.

Number of Hamster Colors

All colors seen in hamsters are not necessarily mutations as some will be re-combinations of existing mutations that create another color. Presently there are about 32 color varieties and coat patterns to choose from and these are listed herewith.

domestic situation, a mutation will eventually appear and when it does it is normally selectively bred for, in order to be preserved. A mutation can happen at any time and in any animal— whether it be a good specimen or a bad one— thus, the latest mutations will generally be seen on hamsters that lack good type. Once they have become well established then breeders will set about improving the quality of hamsters that bear

Coat Patterns & Type

Dalmatian	*Dsdsss*
Piebald	*ss*
Roan	*eeUUWhWh*
Dominant Spot	*DsDs*
Tortoiseshell	*BabaToto*
White Banded	*Baba*
White-bellied Golden	*Whwh*
Angora (Longhair)	*ll*
Satin	*Sasa*
Rex	*rxrx*

Colors and Genetic Formulas

Color		Genetic Formula
Albino		cc
	Pink-eyed	bbc^dc^d
Blond		
	Black-eyed	$LgLgrr$
	Red-eyed	$bbLglg$
Black. Dominant		$eeUU$
Caramel		$bbeeUU$
Chocolate		$eerrUU$
Cinnamon		bb
Cream		
	Black-eyed	ee
	Ruby-eyed	$eeruru$
	Red-eyed	$bbee$
Dove		$dgdg$
Fawn. Ruby-eyed		$ruru$
Guinea gold		rr
Gray		
	Dark	$dgdg$
	Light	$Lglg$
Honey (Amber)		$bbToto$
Ivory		
	Black-eyed	$eeLglg$
	Red-eyed	$bbeeLglg$
Lilac		$bbdgdg$
Sooty		UU
Smoke Pearl		$eedgdg$
White. Black-eyed		$eeWhwh$
Yellow		$Toto$

Albino

The reader will sometimes read of two forms of the albino hamster, one with no dark pigment and one with it. However, there is only

one form of albino and that is the one which totally lacks pigment, is pink-eared and red-eyed. Any white hamster that exhibits dark features, such as ears, eyes or even yellow traces in its fur cannot, by definition, be a true albino. Those with a color such as yellow in the fur are actually very dilute versions of the yellow or other colors where the pigment has been substantially reduced as to appear almost white.

This is a Himalayan hamster with red eyes. This type of hamster is deficient in black coloration, thus the other colors show through.

19

variations of the same genes, so that two breeders might well call a given hamster by differing color names. Most of the color shades are very much heterozygous states and uniformity for color can be achieved only by continual selection for a shade and then breeding for this so that the genes eventually become pure for the shade.

In most animals, albinoism shows variation because at the albino gene locus there is usually a series of possible genes which are arranged in a descending order, from a fully colored individual to the true albino at the bottom of the series. The well-known Himalayan varieties in mice, rabbits, and others are part of this series where partial albinoism is seen.

Blond

These are very light-colored hamsters that look like very pale creams. They are available in black- or red-eyed forms, the latter being somewhat the lighter of the two. It will be found that the colors are somewhat confusing to the beginner because they are actually

Black

A true black has always been the ambition of color breeders but it has not yet been found. Very dark browns and grays have been termed black by breeders but they are actually still only dark examples and not true black. However, it is quite possible that this color will be produced by someone in the future.

Chocolate

This is a nice looking color if it is even. Early chocolates were less than impressive but careful selection has greatly improved the color. However, it still has room for improvement before it reaches the true 'self' color status.

Cinnamon

This color mutation is one of the oldest, having been established in the USA in the mid-to-late 1950's. The color is best described as an orange and while the belly should ideally be white, it is invariably an off-white to cream shade. The eyes are red.

Honey This is a paler version of the cinnamon where a yellowish hue will be seen in the coat. The eyes are red.

Fawn The fawns are not quite as popular as in past years, no doubt because of the progress made by other colors and patterns. In this color will be seen cinnamon, gray, and cream in various mixtures that give the fawn appearance.

Cream

Cream hamsters are always very popular and may have black, ruby or red eyes. The depth of color varies from very dilute to almost apricot and in the show hamster must be even throughout the animal with no areas or hairs in white. The ruby-eyed creams are not an easy variety to breed because the gene for ruby, if in double

A Chinese hamster playing in a tube.

quantity—which it must be to be visual—is linked to sterility in the male. A female must, therefore, be mated to a black-eyed cream male that is split for ruby and the normal expectations will thus be 50% black-eyed and 50% ruby-eyed youngsters—some of the rubies being males. It is the fact that in any one litter males may not appear that means one may give up in frustration at the numbers of young that need to be produced in order to get visual ruby-eyed males.

21

Yellow

The yellow appears somewhat like a very pale orange, darker in the head region, and ticked with black hairs, especially along the back. The eyes are black. This is the only sexlinked color so far developed and this means that the males can exhibit the color when having only a single gene for the color—the alternative gene not being present on the Y chromosome.

Looking down on the top of a Chinese hamster climbing up a wire cage.

Golden

The golden is the original color form and is still very popular. The color is a mixture of orange, brown and black on the back and flanks, this becoming pale to white underneath. The ears are flesh colored through to very dark gray according to the variety, some goldens being more heavily ticked with black than others.

There are darker cheek flashes or stripes and a dark stripe goes from the mid-crown in a line down the back. The extent of this varies considerably. The shoulders and thighs tend also to be more heavily ticked with black so that overall there can be striking contrasts in the way the colors are mixed in the fur. The undercoat is a grayish color and the eyes are black.

White Banded

In this variety a white band encircles the body. Ideally, the line of the band should be straight, but this is very difficult to achieve and most examples will show an irregular line. The width of the band also varies from one animal to the next. White band is inherited independently of the color, so it can be found on all other colors which will be termed cinnamon banded, honey banded and so on, the color referring to the rest of the body and not to the color of the band.

In order to obtain excellent symmetry of the band, one would need to select only the best banded examples to breed from and this would entail disposing of the vast majority of young produced. By the time a consistent degree of uniformity was achieved the degree of inbreeding required would also have stabilized some undesired feature, external or internal, so that one must always beware of these aspects when trying to fix in a given feature.

Tortoiseshell and White

This variety is always a striking hamster, especially if it is a well-marked example, though these are rare. Ideally, the white and two colors that create this pattern should be uniform in size and placement over the body, but this is all but impossible to achieve with any degree of consistency.

Many Chinese hamsters are sold as spotted hamsters.

The mode of transmission of this pattern is sexlinked.

Spotted

In the spotted hamster the color, whatever this is, is dotted with spots of white, though these are more usually blotches of irregular size and shape. Spotted hamsters are really a variation on the skewbald seen in horses, and not to be confused with piebalds where the basic color is white and the patches are

23

colored—the reverse being the case with a skewbald.

The piebald or panda is not often seen but should have patches of color that are clearly defined on the white background color.

Roan

The roan is another of the more recent varieties and here the background color is spotted and flecked with white and gray, giving the roan appearance seen in horses and dogs.

Satin Coat

In the satin coat the hair is fine and silky giving a very characteristic gloss to it. All color varieties have a satin counterpart and this mutation was the first of those which altered the coat type. When pairing a satin it is advisable to match it with a hamster of the same color but carrying the normal coat type as it has been established that paired together the quality of coat in the offspring becomes inferior.

Rex Coat

In the rex mutation, the long guard hairs are reduced to the same size of those of the undercoat which results in a velvet-like look and feel to the fur. In hamsters the rex coat has not achieved the superb texture seen in rabbits but no doubt this will be achieved as time goes by and selection for the best coat types is practiced by more breeders. The rex, as with other coat types, can be combined with any of the color varieties but is possibly best seen in the cream or any variety with minimal undercoat and therefore predisposed to hair which will be totally affected by the rex gene.

Dove and Gray

The dove color is one of the more recent varieties that combines the gray color with a pinkish hue. The gray itself

A pair of colorful hamsters that are satin-coated.

is available as either dark or light, the latter being a silver gray. Both forms carry a blue undercoat. The grays are quite popular as they have good contrast between the areas which have brown and white in them, the darkest hairs being virtually black. The light grays are not unlike another color, the smoke pearl. This is a beige color with streaks of darker hairs in it, mostly on the back and sides, getting lighter as it goes under the belly. The ears are very dark gray to black.

Angora or Longhaired Coat

The mutation for longhair first appeared in the USA and is a relatively recent happening of the mid-1970s. Ideally, the hair should be as long as possible and also dense but these are as yet not fully achieved objectives though examples are getting better all the time. Obviously, the angora haired hamster will need much care of its coat; otherwise it will quickly look unsightly. Grooming must be done gently and regular. Again, all colors are available in angora

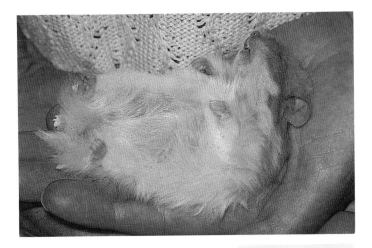

Angora or longhaired hamster.

hair, some looking more attractive than others, but this is a matter for personal decision.

It is to be hoped that as the angora develops it will not go down the same path as so many other longhaired pets do, which is that the hair ultimately is grown to such a length that the poor animal is unable to see properly, and that in order to protect the coat the exhibition specimen is doomed to live on a form of mesh to prevent its coat being soiled or stained. This can be avoided if the various ruling bodies apply a fixed upper limit for coat length.

Hamster Prices

It will be appreciated that the price for a hamster will depend not only on its quality but also on whether it is one of the more unusual colors or hair types. If you plan to breed, then you are strongly advised to stick with well-established varieties while you gain experience as it would be unfortunate if you have problems with varieties that had cost you a good deal more money, and that the problems stemmed purely from lack of experience.

If the hamster is required only as a pet then the first consideration should be for a strong healthy looking youngster—a good hamster is like a good horse; it can never be a bad color.

The smallest of hamster species is *Phodopus sungoris.* This is the satin coated subspecies *P. s. campbelli.*

The small *Phodopus sungoris sungoris* is normally colored like *campbelli*, but it is shown here in its winter coat.

26

STOCK SELECTION

Before going out to buy one or more hamsters, there are considerations concerning the purchase which must not be overlooked. If only a pet is needed, then the local pet shops will have a selection from which to choose—a look into those in your locale should reveal quite a range of colors. If you plan to exhibit or breed specific hamster varieties, then you are better advised to contact a local breeder or visit a hamster farm, as here you will see a wider range and will be able to purchase stock whose genetic state is assured—a matter vital for those planning to breed with their hamsters. Further, even if a pet shop has potentially purebreeding colors, the chances are that the breeders will have retained the best stock for selling themselves.

The next point is that the accommodation should have been purchased in advance of the pet; this is not essential, however, especially if the shop from which you purchase the hamster also has a stock of quality cages—

but this is not always the case—thus the need to treat each aspect separately.

Age

Given the fact that a hamster's lifespan is so short (two to three years) you will certainly want to buy a young animal—ideally six to ten weeks. It can be difficult to tell a young animal from one that is fully mature, though fortunately few shops would try to hoodwink you on this account. A mature hamster will often be larger and such an animal should be individually caged to prevent continuous incidences of fighting. A very young hamster will have fine white hairs just inside its

The normal-coated pygmy *Phodopus s. campbelli*.

ears; these are lost as it matures. The teeth will be very white on a youngster but are likely to yellow as the hamster gets older.

Health

A fit youngster will be constantly inquisitive and on the move but the problem is that hamsters are nocturnal animals and so are often asleep during the day. This means that if disturbed so you can view them, they might not be too frisky.

Eyes

These should be round and clear and show no signs of discharge.

Nose

It should be blunt and show no signs of discharge.

Mouth

There should be no signs of scabs around the mouth and the teeth. In particular the upper and lower incisors should be intact and nicely aligned so that the top just over-reaches but touches the lower.

Ears

These should be clean, as large as possible (such a relative term has value only if you see a number of specimens), and in no way showing signs of having been bitten or having abrasions that could present problems.

Fur

This must be dense and free of any bald spots or signs of parasites. Check under the belly and around the vent area. If the latter is stained this might be due to an excess of greenfood or a sudden change in diet; however, it could indicate 'wet tail' which is usually fatal.

Feet

These should be examined carefully to see that there are no signs of sores. The limbs must be well-formed and free of any signs of deformity.

Transporting Home

It is always better that you take your own carrying box when going to collect a hamster because many pet shops will place the animals in small cardboard boxes from which a hamster could easily escape, if you are not careful. Keep in mind that these little animals can chew through cardboard, and even thin wood, as though it were a piece of carrot! A small plastic container with holes punched in the top, or maybe a biscuit tin with holes in it is the ideal way to secure your new pet: place some suitable bedding in it so the animal is not buffeted about on the homeward journey.

Once installed in its new accommodation, it should be given a light feed of dry foods and then left to explore its new home without being intruded upon by children, who will want to play with their new pet. Parents should be firm and allow children to *watch* but *not touch* during the first day, as it is a stressful time for a hamster changing homes and may be on its own for the first time.

The wild-colored *Phodopus sungoris sungoris*.

The *Phodopus sungoris sungoris* in summer and winter coats.

BREEDING

The breeding of hamsters is a logical step to follow owning one or two as pets, but it should not be undertaken lightly as there are a number of factors which must be given much thought. Firstly, unlike most rodents, hamsters are not social creatures so must be housed in their own accommodation. They are mature at about six to eight weeks so that if one commences breeding then homes must be available for young stock rather quickly or one must have invested in a number of extra cages.

Another point that should be given serious thought is whether the intention is to breed just a few litters a year as potential pets, or whether one wishes to exhibit, or specialize in certain colors and coat patterns. In the former case, while purebreeding stock of good quality is always desirable, it is not as essential as it is in the latter cases. The color breeder and exhibitor will need to maintain a reasonably large stud of

A cream hamster with her 11-day old litter.

hamsters in order to develop their own strains and this will be no inexpensive operation, though most will build up slowly and have developed outlets for unwanted surplus stock. Pet shops will usually buy nicely marked young stock that may not be up to exhibition standard.

The average breeder is unlikely to recover his

Two Chinese dominant spotted hamsters. The lower animal is the male.

overheads so you must not think that your hobby will suddenly become a money spinner; otherwise you will be sadly disappointed.

Breeding Room

It will certainly be helpful if you have a spare room in which your stock can be housed, or maybe you have an outside shed that could be converted into a suitable stockroom. The essentials are that it is draftproof and secure from the entry of mice or rats which will obviously be attracted by the seed and food being stored. The availability of light, heat, and water will certainly make routine jobs that much easier—and more comfortable on those dark winter nights when temperature starts to fall. It is best to supply electric heating which is much the safest option.

In the breeding room there should be a number of shelves to house all of your stock cages and one good working surface on which you can prepare mash foods. Secure metal or plastic containers will be needed to store the extra food purchased in bulk; open sacks are an invitation to rats and mice. A work desk will be useful so that you can study records and plan matings, though these days some breeders are committing their records to home computers which are modestly priced and can bring you information recorded at the touch of a key.

It is advised that breeding operations are kept small until one has gained practical experience. You may find that within a short period you realize that your stock was not up to the needed standard, so it is better to have a low commitment at first and this can be expanded as your knowledge grows.

Sexing Hamsters

Female adult hamsters are usually somewhat larger than males but this is a relative state so is of little use when sexing the animals. If the hamster is gently but firmly secured in your hand, then it can be turned on its back so that the genitals can be inspected. In the female, the anal opening and the genital opening are close together whereas in the male these are further apart. In an adult male, the scrotum containing the testes will be readily seen as small swellings. The males lack the teats of the female—who will normally have seven pairs. The male's underside is more elongated than that of the female but, again, this is not a reliable indicator of the sexes. A good age to sex young stock is from three weeks of age and onward.

Breeding Age

A female is capable of bearing young when she is only about five weeks old but you should not allow such young stock to be mated. The rearing of offspring is very debilitating, and may

Sexing a hamster is not easy for the beginner. The hamster to the left is a female. She is a bit larger than the male and the distance between her anal and genital pores is closer together because her genital pore is usually larger than the male's.

33

result not only in poorly reared youngsters but also in a female that never produces the quality of stock she might have had had she been allowed to mature fully. A good age would be about 12 weeks; if left until she is too old, then the female may either not show interest in being mated or may have become obese, resulting in poorer youngsters. Her breeding life will end when she is about 18 months older.

A male will normally be somewhat slower to mature though he is capable of mating from much the same age as a female. His breeding life is longer than that of the female.

Breeding Condition

Only very fit hamsters should be considered suitable for being paired. Obviously it is not advised that unduly small specimens be used for breeding, nor any that show bad faults of 'type' or have traits that may have a genetic base, such as females who are poor mothers or have a record of attacking their offspring. A poorly fed female, however, may be more inclined towards this latter point than one which is well cared for.

Breeding Cycle

The female is sexually receptive every fourth day and indications of this will be a reddening of her genital area. She will be at her peak during the night, these being nocturnal animals.

Mating

It is most important that the timing of pairs being introduced be exactly right; otherwise the female will most certainly attack the male and may inflict quite nasty wounds. In captivity we have to reverse the situation seen in the wild and introduce the female to the male's living quarters—or have them mate on relatively neutral ground.

If the female is placed in the male's living quarters, he will have an advantage but even so, the pair must be carefully watched. Mutual air sniffing will be the first thing to happen, followed by a grinding of the teeth. The female may then run away and will be pursued by the interested male, or the female may attack the male after the initial contact. In

Facing page: The
male mounts the
female and she
squats to assist him
in his efforts.

Finally in position,
coitus takes place in
a very rapid
succession of
strokes.

such a case, she should be removed and tried again the following evening. If the female that runs away only half attempts to fight the male then she may be about right and if so she will eventually stop and stand quite still, raising her rump end. The male will mate with her very quickly after which he will rest and then mate her again.

The male may well mount the female many times within a short period of time but will eventually become tired and disinterested. The female can now be removed and returned to her own quarters.

A second method of mating procedure is to introduce a male to a neutral breeding box in which a divider can be inserted. After a couple of days, the female can be introduced and the divider inserted so they can see each other, sniff each other but make no other contact (the divider being of mesh). If the female attempts to bite the male through the divider, then leave it in place and by the following night she may be showing signs of 'freezing' when near to her mate. If so, the divider can be removed.

It might seem to the beginner that breeding hamsters sounds a lot of hassle but it is not. It is a case of exercising care in the introduction of pairs—after this things go along without problems in most cases.

It is in fact possible to keep hamster pairs together as long as this state has existed since they were only a few weeks old. There will still be bouts of fighting but they will be less severe than is the normal case when strangers are brought together. However, this is not a natural situation as hamsters are by nature solitary animals and are very happy in this state.

The Birth

The period of gestation in the female is 16 days, though this may sometimes be one, or even two days longer. The baby hamsters are born naked and blind but develop extremely rapidly as fur commences growing after two or three days and the eyes open around the 12th day. Shortly after, the hamsters will be moving around and making their first appearance outside of the nest.

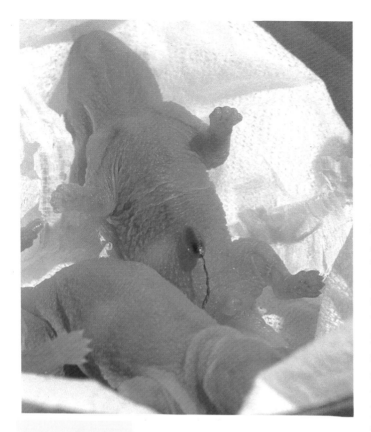

During her lactating period the female will appreciate softfood as discussed in the chapter on feeding; bread soaked in milk will be especially beneficial to her during this period.

Weaning

The process of converting the baby hamsters from their mother's milk to the normal adult diet is known as weaning, and is usually completed by the time they are about four weeks old at the latest. By this time the mother will be tiring of them and may start to attack them so they should be removed to their own stock cage. For as long as they live in harmony, they may be kept together and will play and have mock fights. However, once the fighting becomes for real, then they must all be separated; in any case, the females will be sexually mature by this time so you do not want them to become pregnant. It is advisable to maintain a softfood ration for a few weeks, as well as the normal seed mix, as they will still be growing and in need of extra protein.

The female will be receptive to being mated at

Newly born hamsters about half an hour old. They are born blind, naked and helpless.

During the period of gestation, the female should be disturbed as little as possible and not handled at all as she nears the time of birth. Once the hamsters are born they should not be touched until they are about 14 days old. Should there be need to do so before this time, then rub some of the sawdust or floor covering material on your hands to remove your scent. If this is not done, the female may well kill the babies.

about the time the hamsters are weaned but this is not recommended. Allow her at least four weeks to fully recover from her litter before re-mating her.

Number of Young

The normal litter size will be six to eight though up to 14 may rarely be produced. On such occasions the female will probably kill at least a few of the babies as she has a sixth sense in respect to any that are in any way deformed or not right.

Record Cards

From the moment you purchase a hamster you should give it a record card on which all facts are entered. When hamsters are mated note the date, the period of gestation, the number of young reared, colors, size, markings, how attentive the mother was to the babies, if she attacked any—indeed anything, including apparently unimportant occurrences as these may have significance at a later date. Each youngster should be given a reference number so that you have a complete history of your stud and this can be

used when planning matings.

The card should show any exhibition wins and you should be able to refer as quickly as possible to the success and failures of a given hamster's progeny, this being crucial when assessing the breeding value of a hamster's line.

Fostering

There may be some occasion when it is necessary to foster out babies—maybe the mother has become ill or injured, or has died. If she

A mother golden hamster with her two-week old litter. The babies are weaned by the time they are one month old and they should be removed from the mother. The mother will be biologically able to mate again at this time but it is advisable to give her another month's rest.

39

was of particular merit to your stud, you will not wish to lose her babies and the answer is to place them with another female who has young of the same age, and maybe a small litter.

To achieve this you must, of course, have mated other females at about the same time. The transfer of the babies must be done with great care. Firstly, rub floor dust and the foster mother's urine onto the babies to be transferred and when the foster mother is away from the nest carefully insert the babies among her own. On most occasions she will suspect nothing and all will be well. Occasionally she may be suspicious, in which case rub all over the youngsters again and hopefully she will not know which were hers.

When fostering, it is suggested that in order for you to know which babies are which, you foster to a hamster of a differing color or coat pattern so there are no problems in identification.

Creating Strains

The object of your breeding program is to produce hamsters of a reliable uniformity and of progressively better quality than the stock they were bred from. This is possible only by careful selection of stock retained for breeding, and seeking to remove known faults while doubling up on virtues. This may seem easy enough but has many hidden problems.

Always keep in mind the fact that the best-looking hamster is not necessarily the best breeding hamster. While we endeavor to fix in a quality, we may be fixing in a fault to which it is genetically linked, and not easily separated. We can see only what we are doing to the visual form of our stock—not what we are doing to it internally. So we must monitor matters such as fertility, predisposition to illness, deformities and so on because it is of no gain to have one or two superb animals if they are progressively less fertile or dying of an illness in greater numbers with every few generations.

Inbreeding: Linebreeding

These two methods are

well used, especially when we find a new coat or color mutation in our stock. Linebreeding is merely a more dilute form of inbreeding and for a strain to justify such a title it must be inbred to a greater or lesser degree. In these systems we are trying to retain and increase the number of genes of a given animal or animals in our stock as a whole. To do this, we cannot keep introducing genes from other hamsters of whose breeding qualities we have no clear picture.

One of the advantages of close inbreeding early on in our program is that it will highlight not only the virtues of our stock, but also its failings. If a female hamster received a given feature from both of her parents and her brother did likewise, then no amount of inbreeding to each other will ever produce a negative on that feature. However, if she received a hidden fault on a feature and her brother did likewise, then there is a good chance that fault would show up in their stock if they are paired. This fault, under normal conditions, may have gone unnoticed for a few

generations. Inbreeding thus does not create problems; it merely brings them to our attention rather quickly. If, once we have inbred for two or three generations, we are satisfied we know the faults and virtues of our stock and have, by rigorous selection for the best examples, reduced the incidence of the fault, it is then better we move to a less intense form of inbreeding but one in which we still restrict our pairings to related animals, albeit far more removed. We are now developing a true strain.

Where we will have a problem is if we have got most things right but find the ears of our hamsters are not up to desired standards; how do we go about

41

correcting this without risking the introduction of many unknown factors from another unrelated outcross? The answer is that we select an outcross that has the desired feature, and if this hamster is itself linebred, then so much the better, but this is not vital. What is important is that the chosen hamster excels in its ear carriage *and* has a proven record of siring similar-eared hamsters. This thus indicates a good degree of pureness for this particular feature. Obviously, the chosen outcross must still be sound for its other features.

A male is the better outcross choice simply because he can be mated to a number of females in a relatively short period of time which will enable us to compare the young, to see if he has produced the desired effect. Such outcrossed stock should be monitored carefully before being introduced across the rest of our stud as the male may not have proven as good as we had hoped, in which case we start over again without having his gene lines spread too much in our strain.

The extent to which a true strain can be developed will depend on the number of animals one can keep— progress will be quicker if the numbers are larger—but so will the number of unwanted stock, so we may be governed by the overall economics of the program. It is not enough that we initially purchase excellent stock, nor that we learn as much about breeding theory and genetics, or that we have super accommodation and husbandry; at the end of the day the crucial factor will be our ability to judge what a good hamster looks like, for if we cannot make such a selection, then more often than not the wrong stock will be kept. For this reason the more quality hamsters you can see, the better will be your mental image of what is needed. Breeding is the bringing together of many virtues, each of which has a part to play.

ACCOMMODATION

The three main essentials of a good hamster cage are that it is spacious, contains a nestbox, and is escape-proof. There are today a number of commercially-made hamster homes, many of which are quite good. The ones to avoid are those which are unduly small; some manufacturers are more concerned with getting the right price than with the accommodation best suited for the animal. So merely because small cages are produced, do not be coaxed into believing that their producers know anything about hamsters!

A minimum size would be about 52 × 26 × 26 cm (20½ × 10¼ × 10¼ in) and larger if possible. The nestbox should be about 18 cm (7 in) square, and in order not to take up floor space it is often placed on a shelf in the cage and reached by a ladder type plank. The handy person could, of course, make his own hamster home and if so is able to produce much better units than are produced commercially. Let us

consider a few options in terms of materials.

Wooden Cages

These need to be made of stout timber, say 1.25 cm (½ in) thick and smoothly planed so there are no exposed edges that the hamster can start to gnaw on and thus eventually bite through and escape. Hamsters are very proficient in this particular area! An alternative would be to use one of the coated timbers now available and these have

You can build your own hamster cage, but petshops have such inexpensive cages that it is almost foolish to build your own. This aquarium-style cage was merely set up for photographic purposes. It requires a nestbox to be entirely suitable for a single hamster.

the added advantage that they are much easier to keep clean, needing just a wipe down. Uncoated wood does soak up urine which is its biggest drawback.

The front of a wooden cage can have an all glass sliding window or be of welded wire 2.5 × 1.25 cm (1 × ½ in) hole size and of about 19 gauge thickness. The top could be all wood, hinged for access or it could also be of welded wire—on a frame and also hinged. Because one can make such a home of any size, it follows that it could also incorporate two levels— an upper feeding and playing area and a lower sleeping area which also has additional rooms for use as defecating place and also for hoarding. Thus this is a near replica of the hamster's

natural home. The connection of the upper and lower areas could be via plastic tubes, one at an oblique angle and one almost vertical; these being of slightly differing size (radius), you would be able to tell when the growing hamster had outgrown the smaller diameter tube, which would be ignored and replaced with a slightly larger one. A well-made home such as this could be incorporated into a living room so as to be part of the decor.

Glass or Plexiglas (plastic)
An obvious advantage of glass and plastic is that both are less likely to stain than even coated woods; they are more secure and very attractive. Glass has the further advantage that large aquariums can be used whereas those made with Plexiglas tend to be smaller in size. Again, with the development of silicon rubber compounds, it is possible to build your own all-glass hamster home at a quite modest price. It would be necessary to ensure that the compound is carefully trimmed from all edges so

Nestboxes for hamsters come in many shapes and sizes. Your local petshop can probably show you one that will suit your needs.

the hamster is unable to gnaw on this. Glass is the easier to keep clean over a long period because Plexiglas is prone to being scratched and so eventually takes on a hazy look.

Ecology Cages

If one has a large hamster home, it might be interesting to have it arranged to resemble the hamster's natural real habitat. This type of accommodation is now very popular with aquarists and reptile enthusiasts. There are many sizes of canopies made for aquariums and these will make excellent covers for the top of a cage. They also contain fittings for strip lights and here one can insert a blue night-light. In a darkened room, the activities of the hamster can be watched in light that equates dawn and dusk, when the animals are normally most active. Such a unit would include rocks, sand, and natural branches, together with any other ideas that might prove of interest to the hamster. A visit to the nearest zoo might result in many ideas as most zoos now have specially lighted areas

devoted to nocturnal animals. This is a fascinating area of study that is not yet popular with hamster keepers but which may well become so in the coming years.

Tube Homes

Another type of hamster home that is commercially made is one which comprises a series of tubes connecting various sized circular 'rooms.' These are certainly an excellent idea but their single drawback is that they are rather expensive, the basic kit being very small, which means one must purchase a number of extra tubes and rooms almost immediately. Such units should open into a much larger play area as hamsters do not spend all their time in burrows and dens but forage on the land surface quite a

Nestboxes can be decorative and part of the required gymnastic apparatus necessary to keep your hamster physically fit.

45

lot for food. The various components of such systems could be used to good effect in an ecology cage.

hamster occupied.

When selecting such a home, always take care to check that there are no

Decorative plastic toys, designed for hamsters of very hard, but safe, plastics, are available at most petshops. Hamster love to play with these toys.

All Metal Cages

Most commercially made hamster homes are a combination of sheet metal sides and base with all wire tops. Those which are of a square or oblong shape, all around, are superior to those with sloping tops because they afford more room in which to place wheels and other things to keep the

exposed edges on which the animal could hurt itself. Also check that the paintwork is good, especially in the corners, as here the hamster will tend to defecate. Once the paint peels away, the bare metal will quickly rust and be a constant source of risk of bacterial activities. Should this happen after you have had the cage a while, then it should be scraped down to bare metal and repainted with a non-lead-based paint.

With the greater availability of welded wire panels, one can now make one's own all-wire cages to any size, but the floor should be solid, not wire. The drawback of such cages is they tend to look a bit utilitarian. There are also available wire cages in which the base is of plastic—rather like a cat litter tray, similar to those used in laboratories. These are very hygienic as they can be quickly dismantled for cleaning. Do watch, however, that the hamster does not start to gnaw at the base as, apart from being dangerous, if bits are swallowed, the hamster could escape. This is a recurring warning because these little animals are experts at finding ways of getting out of their home if the opportunity is there.

Food & Water Containers

The most suitable food dishes for hamsters are small earthenware pots which cannot be easily overturned or nibbled as can plastic ones. The gravity type water bottles are preferred by most people rather than open dishes as the water is less likely to be fouled or spilled. It is best to obtain one with an aluminum tip as those of plastic will soon be gnawed, while those which are chromed may become rusty after long use. The water should be changed daily and the ball-bearing checked to ensure it has not become clogged with sawdust or such (which will cause it to drip).

Playthings

Hamsters enjoy playing and should be supplied with a range of interesting objects with which to amuse themselves. Avoid those made of plastic and designed to appeal to you rather than to the hamster! The best things are tubes of cardboard which the animals love to waddle through to investigate; these will eventually be destroyed from nibbling but that is good for the hamster and items such as toilet roll tubes can be made into interesting tunnels at no cost. Pieces of wood, such as empty cotton spools (which also roll) will amuse a hamster and give it something else to chew on.

Small hollowed out logs will also be greatly enjoyed. From these few examples it can be seen that one does not need to spend any money to provide ideal items for the diversion of one's hamster.

Exercise wheels are always a favorite choice with pet owners, and these do give a hamster the opportunity to

Hamsters are born creepers, crawlers and climbers. They are very active, especially when they are hungry. Ladders and trapezes are part of the arse⁻

work off any surplus fat. Some come included in the cage but free-standing models can be purchased. Those for mice are too small. Ideally, obtain one which has solid revolving platform ith struts on it; these are tter than the metal ladder es in which your pet ld accidentally injure its or leg if it got trapped een the metal runners.

There is a great deal of scope both for manufacturers and individuals to devise different ways in which a hamster can exercise itself, yet find it interesting.

Bedding

There are various forms of bedding that can be supplied to a hamster. The best and most practical and readily available will be found in your local pet shop.

Floor Covering

The most used covering for hamster cages is sawdust which can be purchased in large bags from pet shops. Despite its excellent absorbent qualities, it continually sticks to fruit and other food and can create eye problems. Woodshavings from softwoods are less likely to present these latter problems but you will need more to cover the floor as they are less absorbent. Whether sawdust or shavings are used, be sure that the wood it came from has not been treated with chemicals which would be dangerous to the hamster.

Sand is another potential floor covering. As it is less

absorbent than sawdust, it also will need to be deeper layered. Some feel it is rather abrasive for the hamster's feet but the wild hamster has no such problem; pet owners can become over-protective once animals are domesticated. A mixture of sand and clean soil is a very natural surface for a hamster. There is the risk of introducing bacteria with soil and this must be balanced against the benefits the material gives to the hamster as a medium of scratching and digging.

We certainly want to keep our hamsters healthy and not unduly subjected to risk of disease—but we want *them* to be happy as well and be in an environment that most closely equates that which is natural to them. I fear this fact is often forgotten or overlooked by those who seek to ensure that their pets are at risk to nothing, including being contented in their little home.

FEEDING

Hamsters are extremely easy pets to feed as they are very adaptable in their tastes; indeed, a single pet could be fed without any problem just on the contents of a normal kitchen. Essentially, the diet should

Putting a hamster in a small boat and floating it in your bathtub is hardly entertaining to the pet hamster! It is terrified of the water and can easily tip the boat and drown.

comprise the various constituents the body needs in order to function smoothly and maintain resistance to disease. These constituents are carbohydrates to create energy, proteins and fats to promote bodily growth and insulation (they also serve as energy reserves), vitamins to aid metabolic processes and fight off ill health, minerals to create strong bone and aid

Your local petshop has safe toys and cage decorations made especially for hamsters.

other processes and, finally, water to replace any deficit created by evaporation during sweating and by loss through the feces and urine. We will look at a range of foods and discuss their constituents.

Seed

Seed in its various forms will be a major part of a hamster's diet. Seed is divided into two basic groups according to their benefits. Cereal seed, such as wheat, barley, whole or crushed oats, millet of various kinds, and maize are all rich in carbohydrates. Peanuts, sunflower, pine nuts and maw are rich in protein and fat. All seeds contain both minerals and water, protein seeds generally having the higher content by percentage of minerals. The water content of seeds is low but, nonetheless, it is released during the digestive process.

Your hamster should receive mostly *carbohydrate* seeds as the protein seeds will quickly promote obesity—assuming the hamster is otherwise consuming a good portion of other foods. When we talk of seeds in respect to rodents, this can be either in the form of the seeds themselves or in any other form, such as cornflakes, bran, porridge oats, wholemeal bread, cookies, and cakes. Usually a mixture of both types is fed and seen in commercially prepared packets. The contents of popular seeds are shown in the table.

Seeds such as pine nuts can be obtained from pet stores that cater to parrots who especially like these seeds. But any seed can be tried on your hamster if you adopt the basic philosophy that if you can eat it, so can a hamster. Of course, large seeds and nuts such as almonds, Brazil nuts, etc.

COMPARATIVE SEED VALUES BY PERCENTAGE OF CONTENT

Seed	Carbohydrate	Protein	Fat	Mineral
Wheat	74	11	2	2
White Millet	66	12	4	3
Maize	63	10	7	2
Sunflower	21	20	45	3
Peanuts	19	25	45	3
Pine Nuts	12	30	45	4
Maw	12	17	40	6

Note: The above percentages are averages taken from various samplings and will vary depending on area grown, how long stored and other factors.

will need to be crushed to a reasonable size. It must be remembered that all hamsters will not enjoy all seeds so you must establish which are preferred. For this reason, packet seeds are not very economical if you plan to keep a number of hamsters so you are better off to serve these in individual pots to test out which are the most readily taken.

It will be worthwhile, if many hamsters are kept, to test the quality of the seed periodically by germinating some. To do this, simply soak them in cold water for 24 hours, wash them, and then place them on a tray with blotting paper or similar product in the bottom. The tray is placed in a warm, darkened cupboard and after 24 hours, small shoots should appear; if not, try another 12 hours in the cupboard, but if only one or two have germinated by this time, this indicates the quality of the seed is very poor. Sometimes old seed is poor in quality, which is why you don't want to buy too large a supply.

A visit to your local health food store will reveal a whole range of goodies that can be given to your pet as a treat as such stores have many seeds and wholesome products, like mung beans, not always stocked by pet shops and they will all have to be of high quality if for human consumption. Feed only unsalted peanuts to your pet.

Bread that has been cut into cubes and lightly baked in the oven will be appreciated by most hamsters and will give them something to gnaw on—most important with any rodent.

Fruit and Vegetables

Here again, if you can eat it, so can your hamster. Orange, apple, pear, grapes, berries, and raisins are all liked in differing amounts, according to individual tastes. Carrots, spinach, celery, cauliflower, lettuce (the latter has little food value) and the green outer leaves of cabbage, brussels sprouts, etc. are all potential foods for hamsters. Some will partake of little greenfood but most will enjoy various fruits.

All greenfood should be washed before being fed to ensure it does not contain residual harmful chemicals from spraying and general pollution. This is especially true of wild plants such as dandelion, coltsfoot, shepherd's purse, clover, and fresh seeding grasses.

Protein

Beyond the protein contained in the seeds discussed, some amount of protein from animals is of value because seed protein is deficient in certain amino acids (of which proteins are made). Cheese, milk, fish liver oils (usually cod), together with maggots and similar fishbaits can all be offered. If you have a friend who breeds birds, especially canaries or finches, see if they will give you a small amount of their rearing mix to try on your hamster. This is rich in protein and can be purchased from your local pet shop. Mashes however, can be made quite easily by soaking bread in milk or beef stock, adding a drop of cod liver oil, and maybe a few choice seeds. Some cheese and a hard-boiled egg can be added. The whole is pressed firmly to remove excess moisture and then fed to the hamster who will enjoy this occasional treat. Lactating females will gain much benefit from such a mash as at these times they require extra protein for the babies and for their milk production.

In the case of perishable

foods, to avoid flies, pests, and bacteria, only the amount that is quickly consumed should be provided.

Pellets

Commercial rabbit pellets which contain all the ingredients a hamster will need in its diet are often included in hamster mixes and these pellets. A hamster could survive on pellets alone—plus water—but I would never feed such a boring diet to my pets as they have the disadvantage of not providing the hamster with occupational therapy that comes with decisions over what to eat and the simple enjoyment of food. Hamsters certainly enjoy their food, which is easily proven if they are offered a range, including pellets—the latter are often left until last and in the presence of a good range may even be ignored altogether.

Vitamins and Minerals

All of the foods discussed contain vitamins and minerals and providing that the hamster accepts a reasonable range of foods, it is most unlikely it will ever suffer from vitamin or mineral deficiency. The overuse of additives of these compounds can be very dangerous as certain ones are not discharged by the body if in excess, but are absorbed into the tissues where they can then adversely affect other metabolic processes; indeed they can totally counteract the benefits of other vitamins and minerals. If, for any reason, you feel your hamsters are lacking in some way, consult your

veterinarian and explain exactly what diet you feed—this is most important. He can then advise you and prescribe the appropriate additive if this is needed.

Water

If a hamster consumes a

Petshops have pellets and hamster mixes which are balanced diets for hamsters.

regular amount of fruit or vegetables, it will drink very little water as it will get the requisite amount from its diet. However, just to be sure, water should always be available and freshened every day (even if provided via an automatic gravity bottle).

Fussy Eaters

As a result of receiving a very spartan diet in their youth, some hamsters become rather fussy eaters. If this is so, then you need to persevere with known good quality foods. Withhold choice foods for a day (but feed something that they will

Four Paws®

Hamster & Gerbil Brush

Brush your hamster or gerbil daily to remove all unwanted hair this will give them a healthy and beautiful coat.

Item No. 681

Both hamsters and children enjoy the time together during grooming.

eat) and substitute the foods you are trying to persuade them to eat. Obviously, if the hamster just doesn't like the item, persistence is wasted. Fortunately, as stated, this is not a common problem because hamsters are inquisitive eaters, that is, they are always testing new foods.

When to Feed

The best time to supply the daily ration is in the early morning or early evening, though softfoods (mashes and such) are best given in the morning so they can be removed from the cage late in the day. The time is actually unimportant and will generally be which is most convenient. What is important is that it be at a regular time when the hamster will look forward to see if it has anything exciting on that day's menu.

Hoarding

The habit of filling its cheek pouches with food which is then taken to its nest is a natural habit of many rodents. This is no problem except that the hamster will also take perishable foods which can

sour or attract bacteria. For this reason keep an eye on what is being hoarded and reduce the cache to purely seed and other hard foods.

In concluding this chapter, one can say that as the hamster eats so little, comparatively speaking, every effort should be made to ensure the diet is varied and tasty so that your pet will thus be assured of a complete and healthy feeding regimen.

Coprophagy

Rodents practice a double eating process known as coprophagy; it is comparable with rumination in cows and sheep. What happens is that partially digested food is expelled via the anus and immediately re-eaten. These moist pellets are not to be confused with normal fecal pellets containing only waste products. Coprophagy is a quite natural occurrence so do not be alarmed when you see it. The partially digested foods are rich in vitamins which have been synthesized in the lower part of the gut.

GENERAL CARE & HEALTH

If you have provided your hamster with a good spacious cage, and if it is then fed correctly and its home kept nice and clean, then it is unlikely to suffer from any major health problems. However, the more hamsters that are housed in the same building, the greater the risk of illness must be, simply because if one animal succumbs to a complaint, it may quickly spread through the remainder of the stock.

Handling

The first priority with a newly purchased hamster is to hand-tame it so that it can be allowed out of its cage to play, and be carefully examined on a regular basis to see it has no skin complaints, bruises, or other ailments. Handling is essential for any hamster that is to be exhibited, for unless the judge can physically pick it up without having a fight to contend with, the hamster will lose valuable points.

There are three ways of picking up a hamster without subjecting it to discomfort (or loss of dignity).

1. Using both hands you can literally scoop up the hamster onto your palms. This is better employed when the hamster is already hand-tame as otherwise it might panic and jump unless the hands are quickly cupped (in which case it may nip a finger). It is a gentle way to lift up a female that is pregnant or one which is not well.

2. The hand is placed over the hamster so that the thumb and second finger pass around the animal and just in front of its hind legs—the index finger supports its rump and prevents it from backing off. The free hand is placed underneath the hamster. This is the normal way to lift a pet and is used by judges.

3. The hamster can be lifted bodily by grasping the loose skin of its shoulders between your thumb and index finger and then lowered onto your palm. This method is used for restraining a hamster or for handling one that is not fully

tame and liable to bite.

It must be appreciated that a young hamster may nip when first picked up—this is out of fear more than aggression. Once the pet knows it will not be harmed, future handling will never be a problem. This said, hamsters do have periods when they are apparently not in the best of moods and at such times will sit on their haunches and may chatter their teeth, giving clear indication they do not want to be handled. Children *must* be taught to treat their pet with respect and to handle it gently. When it is asleep, it should be left alone—lest you want to end up with a bad-tempered individual!

Once fully tame, a pet hamster will really enjoy walking up your arm, on your shoulder, and on your lap; they are very inquisitive creatures so are always on the move. Care must be taken when they are on the arms of chairs, or any high surface, as they are liable to jump from these with the risk of injury. They are rather short-sighted so are not always aware how far down they will drop.

When your hamsters are loose, cats and dogs should be kept clear of them as they are natural enemies of all rodents. The fact that cats and dogs have been known to live happily with a loose hamster means absolutely nothing, for only one moment of excitement can result in tragedy for your little pet—at best it might receive a bad mauling.

Another point to watch is that the hamster does not disappear behind or under skirting boards or heavy furniture whence it cannot be collected. Should this happen, then place some favored tidbits near the last seen place and maybe it will be lured out. If not, place the cage at that spot in the hope that it will eventually find its way back and enter the cage to feed and sleep.

Siting a Cage

Never place a hamster cage where it will be directly in the path of sunshine as these animals are nocturnal and will quickly suffer from heatstroke if exposed. Likewise, they will quickly become chilled if exposed to a draft. The best place for the cage is, therefore, in a corner or by a wall adjoining

a door rather than one facing it. Place it at a reasonable height so you can see into the cage without the need to bend.

Herbal Tonics

Although we live in an age when highly sophisticated drugs, antibiotics, and other preparations are commonly used to cure most ailments in both ourselves and our pets, nonetheless, there is still a very strong case for the use of old fashioned tonics made from herbs. These have extra benefit to rodents and lagomorphs (rabbits and hares) where certain bacteria are essential to the digestive process. In these animal groups, the use of antibiotics is not without risk, for such treatments, while killing detrimental bacteria, invariably destroy needed and beneficial protozoans as well. When this happens, the animal is vulnerable to attack by other bacteria. Herbal tonics can be purchased from some pet stores but will be found in greater numbers in health food shops; there is growing interest today in homeopathy which, when prescribed correctly, has no negative side effects as do many of the modern drugs. Most herbal tonics stem from very common plants such as dandelion, clover, blackberry, chickweed, plantain, groundsel and the most well-known of all, garlic. The real herbal enthusiast can easily make his own tonics by boiling the plants in water, straining off the plant, and allowing the liquid to cool. The degree of concentration will be determined by the amount of water used. Those interested in this aspect of husbandry are recommended to purchase a good herbal book which will detail many plants, their properties, and the ways in which they can be used.

Health Matters

An unwell hamster is not difficult to spot as it will sit hunched up and move about in the same manner. Its fur will appear dull and 'stand off' the skin. Its feces will be unusually liquid and may be very green in color. However, on this latter point, due consideration may be given to the diet and a hamster may have green, moist feces because it has eaten a lot of greenfood, so the general health will indicate whether this is serious or not. In such cases, simply reduce the amount of greenfood given.

A runny nose or weeping eyes usually indicate a chill, but if this does not clear up within a day or two, then a more serious complaint must be considered, of which these two signs are symptomatic. One of the major problems in treating small animals is that they often die before the cause is known. Diarrhea is a clinical sign of a vast range of diseases so unless treatment is prompt, the animal then develops secondary infections resulting from its reduced ability to fight off the first infection or disease.

At the first signs of a problem, isolate the hamster and apply heat treatment via an infra-red lamp which can be attached to a hospital cage. These lamps are relatively inexpensive yet are the best 'cure-all' investment a breeder can make. Minor colds, together with a whole range of other disorders, can be nipped in the bud simply by applying heat and reducing the diet to seed and water. The lamp is so placed that the hamster can move in or out of the heat source as it desires. It should then be left in total quietness away from other stock and especially from children.

Once recovered, it should be acclimatized back to its normal cage temperature; otherwise it will simply become ill again from chilling. If an infra-red lamp is not owned, then a lightbulb suspended above a cage will be better than nothing. The temperature needs to be maintained at about 25°C (77°F) and then steadily reduced in relation to recovery. If an animal has been subjected to heat treatment, then it should not be taken to the vet at that point; otherwise any benefits gained will be lost. In any event, it is wise to consult your veterinarian the minute more than a minor chill or digestive upset is suspected. Lamps used should not be so close to the cage bars that they heat them so that the hamster could burn itself on them. An overhead fixture is, therefore, the best.

Quarantine

Should you already own one or more hamsters, then

any fresh additions to your stock should be quarantined for a period of not less than 14 days—21 days would be better. Over such a period, any illness being incubated would normally show itself. If the hamster is still well at the end of this period, it can then be placed into the stockroom with other hamsters.

Wet Tail

This is *the* disease most feared by hamster owners as it is both highly contagious and nearly always fatal to the animal. It is caused by an infection in the intestine and the name derives from the wet fur around the anal region, not to be confused with diarrhea. If your vet confirms this disease, then all bedding material must be destroyed and wooden cages burnt. Metal cages can be subjected to a blowtorch. This rather drastic action is the only way you can reduce the risk of your other stock becoming infected. Should a hamster recover from the complaint, it should never be used for breeding as the full workings of this problem are not yet understood. The fact that certain animals seem to have an existent resistance while others do not gives veterinarians reason to suspect the existence of a genetic base.

Pouch Complaints

Should a sharp food item or wood shavings puncture the delicate lining of a hamster's mouth pouch, an abscess can develop. You will notice that the hamster's pouch appears swollen although the animal is not filling it. This is possibly accompanied by the weeping of an eye. Treatment must be rapid by your vet if any success is hoped for. Avoid food items like a spike of oats which can have sharp pieces on them.

Greasy Fur

You may sometimes notice that your pet has what appears to be spots of grease or oil at the sides of its flanks but these are quite natural and is a secretion from the scent glands. These serve to identify individuals and their territory and are more prominent in the male than the female. The hamster will rub itself against the cage sides and any residue will be removed as the hamster grooms itself.

Teeth Problems

It has already been mentioned in an earlier chapter that the teeth of rodents, or specifically those of the front—the incisors—are growing continually. Should they be out of line, then they will not wear down as they should and could thus cause problems of feeding. In such cases they can be trimmed back by your vet, and thereafter will need to be watched, and probably trimmed again at a later date. Obviously such hamsters must not be bred from even though in a particular instance the problem may have stemmed from an incorrect diet early in life of the hamster—but you cannot be sure.

Hibernation

Should the ambient temperature of a hamster's home drop below a certain figure this then will induce a semi-hibernation, or torpid state. If the hamster does not wake up as it normally does, you could even suspect it is dead, and in order to revive the animal to its normal state the temperature should be increased in the room.

There are, of course, numerous other ailments which can afflict your pet but under normal conditions those discussed herein are the most likely. The hamster, being a solitary animal, is probably healthier—or at least at less risk to disease—than most pets, always providing you look after it in the manner detailed in the various chapters of this book.

As your pet gets older you may notice that its hair starts to come out and bare patches may result—we all have this to face so it should not be the cause for worry—only if the bare patches appear red and sore. Again, an old hamster is more prone to tumors and their removal will not normally be possible so it is a case of deciding among the family if the animal is in undue pain or not. If it seems fine, then hopefully it will simply die of old age but if not, then you may need your vet to painlessly end its short but happy life.

63

Index